You've Got Hate Mail

by Billy Van Zandt
and Jane Milmore

A SAMUEL FRENCH ACTING EDITION

FOUNDED 1830
NEW YORK HOLLYWOOD LONDON TORONTO
SAMUELFRENCH.COM

Copyright © 2007, 2010 by Billy Van Zandt Living Trust
and Jane Milmore Living Trust

ALL RIGHTS RESERVED

Cover Art & Graphic: Noel Kubel

CAUTION: Professionals and amateurs are hereby warned that *YOU'VE GOT HATE MAIL* is subject to a Licensing Fee. It is fully protected under the copyright laws of the United States of America, the British Commonwealth, including Canada, and all other countries of the Copyright Union. All rights, including professional, amateur, motion picture, recitation, lecturing, public reading, radio broadcasting, television and the rights of translation into foreign languages are strictly reserved. In its present form the play is dedicated to the reading public only.

The amateur live stage performance rights to *YOU'VE GOT HATE MAIL* are controlled exclusively by Samuel French, Inc., and licensing arrangements and performance licenses must be secured well in advance of presentation. PLEASE NOTE that amateur Licensing Fees are set upon application in accordance with your producing circumstances. When applying for a licensing quotation and a performance license please give us the number of performances intended, dates of production, your seating capacity and admission fee. Licensing Fees are payable one week before the opening performance of the play to Samuel French, Inc., at 45 W. 25th Street, New York, NY 10010.

Licensing Fee of the required amount must be paid whether the play is presented for charity or gain and whether or not admission is charged.

Stock licensing fees quoted upon application to Samuel French, Inc.

For all other rights than those stipulated above, apply to: Sendroff & Baruch, LP, 1500 Broadway, Suite 2001, New York, NY 10036 Att: Mark Sendroff.

Particular emphasis is laid on the question of amateur or professional readings, permission and terms for which must be secured in writing from Samuel French, Inc.

Copying from this book in whole or in part is strictly forbidden by law, and the right of performance is not transferable.

Whenever the play is produced the following notice must appear on all programs, printing and advertising for the play: "Produced by special arrangement with Samuel French, Inc."

Due authorship credit must be given on all programs, printing and advertising for the play.

ISBN 978-0-573-69772-2   Printed in U.S.A.   #29201

No one shall commit or authorize any act or omission by which the copyright of, or the right to copyright, this play may be impaired.

No one shall make any changes in this play for the purpose of production.

Publication of this play does not imply availability for performance. Both amateurs and professionals considering a production are strongly advised in their own interests to apply to Samuel French, Inc., for written permission before starting rehearsals, advertising, or booking a theatre.

No part of this book may be reproduced, stored in a retrieval system, or transmitted in any form, by any means, now known or yet to be invented, including mechanical, electronic, photocopying, recording, videotaping, or otherwise, without the prior written permission of the publisher.

MUSIC USE NOTE

Licensees are solely responsible for obtaining formal written permission from copyright owners to use copyrighted music in the performance of this play and are strongly cautioned to do so. If no such permission is obtained by the licensee, then the licensee must use only original music that the licensee owns and controls. Licensees are solely responsible and liable for all music clearances and shall indemnify the copyright owners of the play and their licensing agent, Samuel French, Inc., against any costs, expenses, losses and liabilities arising from the use of music by licensees.

IMPORTANT BILLING AND CREDIT REQUIREMENTS

All producers of *YOU'VE GOT HATE MAIL must* give credit to the Author of the Play in all programs distributed in connection with performances of the Play, and in all instances in which the title of the Play appears for the purposes of advertising, publicizing or otherwise exploiting the Play and/or a production. The name of the Author *must* appear on a separate line on which no other name appears, immediately following the title and *must* appear in size of type not less than fifty percent of the size of the title type.

YOU'VE GOT HATE MAIL opened May 25, 2007, at the Brookdale College Performing Arts Center, in Lincroft, New Jersey, under the direction of Billy Van Zandt and Art Neill. It was produced by Noel Kubel and Jack Ryan. Set design was by Noel Kubel. Light and sound design were by Chris Woolley. Photography was by Danny Sanchez. The stage manager was Lauren Cervasio.

RICHARD	Billy Van Zandt
STEPHANIE	Jane Milmore
PEG	Sherle Tallent
GEORGE	Glenn Jones
WANDA	Darcy Bagnasco

YOU'VE GOT HATE MAIL opened Off-Broadway at the Triad on June 25, 2010, under the direction of Gary Shaffer. It was produced by Billy Van Zandt, Gary Shaffer, and Jane Milmore. Associate Producer was Noel Kubel. Stage Manager was Jen Lucero. Photography was by Danny Sanchez. Graphic art was by Noel Kubel. The cast was as follows:

RICHARD	Billy Van Zandt
STEPHANIE	Jane Milmore
PEG	Barbara Bonilla
GEORGE	Glenn Jones
WANDA	Fran Solgan

Standbys: For Billy Van Zandt and Glenn Jones, Jeff Babey; For Stephanie, Rebecca Harris Flynn; for Peg, Bonnie Deroski; for Wanda, Allison Foote.

CHARACTERS

RICHARD
STEPHANIE
PEG
GEORGE
WANDA

AUTHORS' NOTES

This play can be performed on a bare stage with five tables and chairs, or an elaborate set with isolated lighting.

It can be rehearsed like a regular play, or staged with five actors reading their scripts off the laptops live. Unlike *Love Letters* we want the person receiving each email to react in real time, as well as the person who is reading what they are writing – reaction is the name of the game here.

No one should make eye contact with another actor until the curtain call – perform in your own area. Adding a little staging at each actor's station is encouraged time-to-time (e.g George hiding under the table when he hides under his bed, etc). Especially during the Blackberry and iPhone pieces when it's nice to stand up.

Please don't add excessive props, or costume changes.

Each actor's station should contain nothing more than their laptop, their iPhone or Blackberry, and their drink.

The men should wear suits, and the ladies should wear appropriate "office/cocktail-wear." Please don't get caught up in the clicking of the keyboards, or in staring down as you type.

Final Note: Due to the language and themes we advise the play be advertised as "For Mature Audiences" or something of that nature. It will also sell more tickets.

–Billy Van Zandt &
Jane Milmore

(An empty stage.)

(The play is presented without an intermission – as intimately as possible. There is no curtain. A backdrop simulates a giant computer monitor.)

(In the glow of the monitor's screensaver, five actors enter from the same side of the wings and take seats at their laptops.)

(They turn them on. We hear various start-up noises:)

COMPUTER VOICES/NOISES. You've got mail/Mail truck!/You've got mail.

(The last noise we hear is dial-up.)

(As each actor types his or her e-mails and speaks for the first time, lights come up full on him or her and remain so until otherwise indicated in the script.)

RICHARD. Wanda, OK. My turn. I'm picturing you in your tight orange shirt with the snaps up the front. You see me watching you, so you begin teasing me, taunting me, brushing your breasts up against me in the copy room. I can feel your nipples right through my sweater vest. I can't stand it any longer, so I rip the shirt right off your body while Linden the security guard spies on us from behind the shredder. And as I bury my face in your huge mountains of love, I bang your brains out on top of the copier, xeroxing your tight 23 year-old ass as we go!

WANDA. Mmmmmm. Ooohhhh. Richard…! Yeeesss. YEEEEEESSSS-IN CAAAAAAPPPPPPPPPS…!! I'm so excited I can't stand it. I'm getting wet just thinking about you. I'm pulling up my skirt. Christ, my nipples are so hard, I…Hold on, I have to sign for a Fed Ex package.

STEPHANIE. Dear Peg. Look what my adorable husband Richard bought me! My own wireless computer! I have no idea what I'm doing. But I'm loving it. And I have so many new friends. I got 52 e-mails the second I turned it on. The weird thing is most of them want to sell me a penis enlargement.

PEG. Stephanie, don't answer those. That's spam! And stop using capital letters. It means you're screaming.

STEPHANIE. Says who?

PEG. Whoever started all this.

STEPHANIE. Al Gore?

(**PEG** *laughs.*)

PEG. Yes. Al Gore. LOL.

STEPHANIE. What's LOL?

PEG. "Laughing. Out. Loud."

STEPHANIE. Why don't you just write "Ha ha?"

PEG. Too many letters.

(**STEPHANIE** *reacts.*)

PEG. What year are you living in? Jeez Stephie, since you married Richard you've become a real Stepford Wife.

STEPHANIE. He likes it. And I can't help it. I guess that's what happens when you're married, Peg. You'll see.

PEG. Not at the rate I'm going. Last night – another loser date. I don't know why I even bother at this point.

STEPHANIE. But he's an architect, like you. I thought you liked him on the phone.

PEG. I did. Then I met him in person for a drink. And boy, he couldn't get out of there fast enough. Kept looking at my ass and shaking his head. Like he was a prize package. He had bigger breasts than I do.

STEPHANIE. At least this one stayed for the drink. Was this from Match.com or eHarmony?

PEG. Neither. One of my clients set us up. "He's great." "You'll love him." Yeah. Wait until I re-design my client's bathroom plumbing. Then we'll see who gets shit on next time!

WANDA. OK, baby. I'm back. Ooooohhh. Yeeessss. Oh, yesss! Oh, Richard! You're making me CRAZY-IN-CAPS!!! I want you to drag me naked by my hair past Linden and the copier up to the conference room where you force me to do you in front of all the junior partners in the middle of a board meeting! Oh, God, I can't wait until 5:00!

RICHARD. Me, either. Meet me in the men's room on the fourth floor. Our stall. You be the lady with the plumbing problem, and I'll be the dirty janitor.

STEPHANIE. *(brightly)* Hi, Richard. It's me, Stephanie.

RICHARD. Ah!

STEPHANIE. What's up?

RICHARD. *(freezes for a moment, then)* Nothing. Hi, honey. Really busy at work here. Sort of got my hands full.

STEPHANIE. Just want to tell you I love my new computer. I'm learning so much. I just Googled myself. According to them I'm a cellist from Julliard with Celiac's disease.

RICHARD. That's great, honey.

RICHARD. *(his voice deepening as he types a second e-mail)* Wanda, I'll be there in five minutes, you dirty, filthy slut. Don't forget to bring the ruler that jams the door shut.

STEPHANIE. Hi, sweetie. It's me, again. Stephie.

RICHARD. Ah, come on!

STEPHANIE. I love being able to communicate with you whenever I want. So what do you think I should do – at the Red Cross Ball, should I seat the Vassers and the Brewsters together after that whole stock thing?

*(**RICHARD** is frustrated and wants to get her off the computer.)*

RICHARD. Whatever you want, baby. Love talking to you too, but remember this is my job. Have to go. Working late tonight. Don't bother e-mailing me back – I'm in meetings all day. Love you.

WANDA. Hot stuff, hope I caught you in time. The bathroom is off limits. That creepy almost-a-midget cleaning woman is in there and it reeks of ammonia and Fritos.

RICHARD. Damn it!

(**STEPHANIE** *reacts to the following.*)

RICHARD. Just as well. I was supposed to be in court a half hour ago. I'll meet you at the hotel bar.

STEPHANIE. *(staring at screen)* Huh?

RICHARD. Let some guy buy you a drink, get his hopes up, and then I'll come in, pretend I don't know you, order you to stand up and take off your panties right there in front of everyone and then make you follow me to the elevator where we can do it on the way up to the hotel room. Til 5:00, my little Brazilian wax job. Stay wet, Richard.

STEPHANIE. *(staring at screen)* Ewww!

WANDA. Richard, why did you send me that e-mail? What do you mean you have meetings all day and have to work late? I already booked the room!

(**RICHARD** *looks at his SENT file and freaks, rising up and grabbing his head.*)

RICHARD. Oh, no! Oh, God! Oh, shit!

STEPHANIE. Richard? That last e-mail made no sense. And how do you know I'm wet? I was talking to Reynaldo while he was cleaning the koi pond and that big fish with the weird eyes splashed water all over me. Is there a camera in this thing?

(no response)

STEPHANIE. Richard? Are you there?

(no response)

STEPHANIE. Peg, what do you make of this? I just got this creepy e-mail from Richard. See below:

PEG. Thanks. I just threw up in my mouth. Why would you send that to me? Some things you never want to picture. And right now my top three are my parents screwing, Brad Pitt sitting on a toilet, and Richard getting off on his laptop.

STEPHANIE. Ewww, he'd never do that.

(**PEG** *reacts, as if to say, "Yeah, sure."*)

STEPHANIE. You know something? There's another address at the top of the screen above mine. I don't think it was intended for me.

PEG. No shit, Sherlock. Richard's a piece of crap who has been cheating on you since your wedding night. Best thing you could do is smother him with a dry cleaning bag.

(**PEG** *goes to sip her Starbucks.*)

PEG. I can't send that. Delete.

(*She deletes it all and retypes.*)

PEG. Stephanie, yeah that's weird. Must be some sort of office joke.

(**PEG** *buries her face in her hand and awaits the response.*)

GEORGE. Richard, I don't normally send these, but this one's funny. Click on the link. It's a fat kid screaming as he falls out of a Ferris wheel.

RICHARD. George. Help. Oh, Jesus. Help. I screwed up. I just sent Stephanie an e-mail that was supposed to go to Wanda.

GEORGE. Was it the screaming fat kid falling out of the Ferris wheel?

RICHARD. No! This is bad.

GEORGE. How bad can it be?

RICHARD. Here.

(**GEORGE** *reads and reacts.*)

GEORGE. HMOG!

RICHARD. What's HMOG?

GEORGE. Holy Mother of Christ! That's pretty bad. You're doing the fourth-floor receptionist with the great rack and the bad skin?

RICHARD. She doesn't have...Thanks, you're about as helpful as the pimples on your ex-wife's ass.

GEORGE. I'm sorry I ever told you that.

RICHARD. Stephanie, sorry if you got any weird e-mails from my computer. The new guy down the hall...Hal something...he was on my computer while I was in the bathroom and he sent out some x-rated e-mails to someone that I don't know or ever met in my entire life. I think one of them went to you by mistake. It's hard to explain how it works, but trust me, it happens all the time with these darn computers. Make sure you delete it. We wouldn't want something like that on our home computer.

RICHARD. Wanda, sorry for the confusion with the e-mail. That was for my wife. I'll see you at the bar. Picturing you commando, Richard.

STEPHANIE. Peg, I feel so stupid. Richard explained that disgusting e-mail was written by a guy – Hal Something – from his office. What a creep. Using someone else's computer so he doesn't get caught writing nasty things. Don't you think the man who wrote that is sleazy?

PEG. Yes, I do.

(**PEG** *reads the e-mail looking for an address.*)

PEG. Let me see that. You cc'd your wife, you jag off. Nice screen name. "Iwandadoit69."

(**PEG** *types.*)

PEG. Dear Wanda. Hi, it's me, Richard. Remind me what bar we're meeting at.

(pauses, then)

Stay wet, Richard.

WANDA. What do you mean "what bar?" It's Thursday, isn't it? The Nat King Cole Room at the St. Regis. What's wrong with you today? And what e-mail address is this you're writing from? "Art-B-4-Function?" Who is "Art-B-4-Function?"

PEG. I'm at the computer of a new guy down the hall. Named Art. He sits right B-4...Hal Function. Another new guy. You don't know him. Had to move. "You-know-who" keeps looking over my shoulder, so I had to find another computer.

WANDA. You know, you should fire that assistant of yours. She's always checking up on you. Plus, she thinks she's so much better than me – with her Manalo shoes and her dry-cleaned clothes. UOK, baby? U don't even sound like yourself.

PEG. *(panics, then)* Don't make me have to spank you in front of all the people at the bar tonight. Bitch.

WANDA. That's my Richard! Yeah, I think you may have to spank me, Daddy. I've been thinking very bad things all day long. What about you, Richard? Are you thinking of terrible things, too?

PEG. Oh, yes. I'm thinking of terrible things happening to Richard right now.

WANDA. Like what? Tell me every naughty detail.

*(**PEG** moans with displeasure as she starts to type.)*

PEG. Okay. When I least expect it, I want you to take a broomstick and shove it up my ass, spin me around like a candy apple, slapping me the entire time, while calling me your stupid bitch.

WANDA. OOOOOOOOOOOOOOOOOOOOOHHHHHHHHHHHHHHHHHHHH!!

RICHARD. Good morning, Stephie-pie. I didn't have the heart to wake you when I finally got in last night. You were smiling in your sleep so I knew you were dreaming about me. Tonight you get the real thing, sugar. Oh. See if you can get my dry cleaning before I get home. I don't know what's happening lately. I'm going through shirts like you go through decorators.

STEPHANIE. Richard, cutie. Will pick up your shirts after I get your clubs re-gripped, then it's lunch with your mother. Thanks for the box of chocolates. You sure they were for me? Five pieces were already eaten when I opened the box.

(**RICHARD** *reacts.*)

WANDA. Hey there, Beastie Boy. Last night was wild. I can barely walk today. And, by the way, you were a naughty boy for taking the rest of my chocolates. You'll need to be punished for that.

RICHARD. Do what you have to do. Just lay off the broomstick, will ya? That was just weird.

WANDA. OK. But write me another e-mail like the one you sent me yesterday. That's the hottest cybersex we ever had. I had to put my hand over my mouth by the time I got to the end.

(**RICHARD** *has no idea what she's referring to, but starts typing anyway.*)

PEG. Stephanie, I don't know how to tell you this. Believe me, I thought about it for a very long time. And, well, I think this is the right thing to do. Attached are a few pictures I took in a bar last night. I think these photos speak more clearly than anything I could say. I'm sorry to have to show this to you. I love you. And I'm here for you. Call me as soon as you open these.

STEPHANIE. Peg. I can't open this. What is it? Another YouTube video of David Hasselhoff drunk? I asked you to stop sending me those.

PEG. Not quite. Double click on the red icons. And Stephanie…I'm really sorry.

STEPHANIE. What is –

(*She is stunned.*)

STEPHANIE. Oh God. Oh my God!! I can't…I can't breathe.

(**PEG** *pleads with the screen for an answer to her e-mail. None comes.*)

PEG. Stephanie? Are you there?

STEPHANIE. Richard, what the hell is this?!

RICHARD. What the hell is what?

STEPHANIE. Sorry. Forgot the attachment. Here!

(**RICHARD** *spits out his coffee.*)

RICHARD. Oh, no. Oh, God.

STEPHANIE. Richard? I know you're there. You're on my buddy list. Didn't think I knew what that was, did you? Answer me!

RICHARD. George, look what Peg sent to Stephanie! Can you believe that sea turtle? That big bucket of pig slop!

GEORGE. Is that girl taking her panties off right in the bar? Wow. That's hot. That's a keeper. P.S. – her skin doesn't look so bad in this shot.

RICHARD. Honey, of course I'm here. Don't worry. I know what happened. It's Linden the Security Guard. That crazy knucklehead. He does this all the time. He takes people's heads and put them on other people's bodies. As a joke! You should see the obviously fake nude Hillary Clintons he sent me. I'll send them to you. You will laugh.

STEPHANIE. Liar! That picture is from Peg's cell phone. She was in the bar last night.

RICHARD. Stephanie, a client's on the line. I'll get right back to you.

RICHARD. Peg, thanks for sabotaging my marriage, you hateful lump of shit.

PEG. Dear Richard, eat me. I knew your marriage was over when you grabbed my ass at your wedding.

RICHARD. When was that? Back when you were a hundred pounds lighter? I could never do that now. Because I don't carry around a forklift, you fat slob. Do you realize what you've done?

PEG. Do you realize what YOU'VE done?

STEPHANIE. Richard, stop calling me. I'm not going to answer the phone. I don't want to hear the sound of your voice. Who is this woman?

RICHARD. Calm down. I'm on my way home. She's nobody. A client. It was a business meeting. That's all. An innocent business meeting. I'm a lawyer. I meet clients in bars all the time.

STEPHANIE. She's taking off her panties. And you're kneeling in front of her.

RICHARD. Because that's what the court case is all about. She was demonstrating how she did this with an old boyfriend when they arrested her for no apparent reason.

STEPHANIE. Really? Check out the second picture, you lying bastard.

RICHARD. *(to himself)* How the hell did Peg get in the elevator?

PEG. Stephanie? Richard just wrote me. Are you all right?

GEORGE. Richard, HMOG, are you in trouble. I can't stop looking at this picture. Any chance she sent you more than one photo? If so, send them to me immediately. P.S. – here's another Hillary Clinton.

RICHARD. Enjoying your cell phone camera, Peg? Next time I see you, I'm gonna shove it up your gargantuan ass. Just because your life is miserable you have to make everyone else's life miserable, too, you toxic piece of home-wrecking shit?

PEG. Wanda, just found out I have crabs, You may want to see a doctor. Love, Richard.

(WANDA reacts.)

STEPHANIE. Richard does this…this…slut work with you? How do you know her? Does she know you're married? What am I saying? How could you do this?

RICHARD. Jesus, Stephanie, I love you. You're my whole life. I'm so sorry. I really screwed up.

WANDA. Screw you, Richard. You didn't get crabs from me! Check your wife!

RICHARD. Wanda, I don't know what the hell you are talking about. Something's come up. I'll meet you at the restaurant.

RICHARD. I swear, Stephanie. She took advantage of me. Remember how vulnerable I was after your grandmother died. You were so cold and distant.

STEPHANIE. I was in Wyoming!

RICHARD. Exactly. And remember while you were gone I won that big case and you sent that bottle of Cristal to my office to congratulate me? Well, before I knew it, this terrible woman used it to get me drunk and take advantage of me. Like Demi Moore in that movie with Michael Douglas. You love that movie, remember? He was the good guy. She was the bad girl. I think that's out on DVD now.

STEPHANIE. What are you talking about!?

RICHARD. I don't know. Jesus, Stephanie. I'm so sorry. I'm coming home right now. I love you.

STEPHANIE. Oh my God, she does work there! Then everybody at Ryan, Murphy and Kubel, knows?! Who is she? What's her name?

RICHARD. I don't know, I can't remember. Wanda something.

STEPHANIE. Have I met her? How old is she?

RICHARD. Not as old as you, I promise. You've never met her. She's not allowed on this level. She's purely fourth floor. She's nothing. She answers phones. A monkey can do that.

STEPHANIE. Then why??!!

RICHARD. I don't know. I think I need rehab.

STEPHANIE. Are you going to fire her?

RICHARD. I can't. It's not my department.

STEPHANIE. What do you mean, "It's not your department?" You're about to become a partner!

RICHARD. Yes, but…she's black, and that could get me into a whole thing…

STEPHANIE. She's not black. I'm looking at pictures of her!

RICHARD. Yes, but that was after damn Linden changed the skin tones in the pictures. For God's sake, I look like a

Norwegian albino. That damn Linden. I'm firing him! I don't care if he IS black.

STEPHANIE. Stop doing that! I already know Peg took the pictures, you idiot!

RICHARD. Sorry Steph, that last comment was made by the new guy from down the hall – Hal Somebody. I'm coming home right away. We'll sort this all out. This isn't as bad as it looks. I'm sure we'll be laughing about this in an hour.

(lights down)

(lights up on **STEPHANIE***)*

STEPHANIE. Dear Peg, if you need me I just checked into the W Hotel in Union Square. Don't tell anyone where I am. Oh, Peg. Richard came home and it was awful. It felt so unreal. He kept saying he was sorry and I kept screaming and throwing things at him. He has a lump on his head from where I hit him with his golf trophy. I ran out while he was laying there bleeding.

PEG. Stephanie, oh God. Are you all right? I feel so awful for you. I always swore I would never get involved in someone else's private affairs. But when I saw the two of them in that bar it seemed so public. I felt humiliated for you and I got so angry. I hope I did the right thing.

STEPHANIE. I can't trust a thing he says. I want to hurt him like he hurt me. I want to sleep with Derek Jeter and make him watch. He keeps calling my cell phone but I won't answer it. I just want to go to sleep and wake up and find out this was all a bad dream.

PEG. If you need anything let me know. I have some Ambien and a bottle of Grey Goose.

STEPHANIE. I can't believe three hours ago I was making a pot roast.

(**WANDA** *types into her BlackBerry.*)

WANDA. Richard, where are you? I've been waiting here for hours and your cell phone goes right to messages.

Are you okay? You know I hate waiting alone in restaurants. People are looking at me like I'm a hooker or something. I'm freezing my ass off. Ten more minutes and I'm putting my panties back on.

RICHARD. George? This is a nightmare. She left me, man. I don't know what to do.

GEORGE. Who left you? "Bad skin?" Or Stephanie?

RICHARD. Stephanie. I came home to apologize and she went berserk. She called me names. She threw things at me. Tossed my clothes out the bedroom window. Turned on the sprinklers. And drove off into the night with me laying there with a little silver golf club sticking out of my forehead. What kind of person just walks out after ten years? Isn't everyone entitled to one mistake? Besides, everybody does it. I just got caught.

GEORGE. I never did it. I don't know anyone who HAS done it. Just you.

RICHARD. That's crap. You flirted all the time when you were married.

GEORGE. Flirting is not the same thing as hanging naked from a chandelier in a hotel room while some slut in hostess pants and a turban whips you with a towel.

RICHARD. What?

GEORGE. Nothing.

WANDA. Dear Art, you don't know me, but I know you're the new guy on Richard's floor and you let Richard use your computer. Have you seen him?

PEG. Yes, I see him right now. He's over by the candy machine, shitting himself at the thought of ever having boinked you. "Boinked," as in "oinked," you pig.

(**PEG** *laughs. She scores one for herself.*)

WANDA. Who the hell is this? I swear to God, I'll kick your ass.

RICHARD. George, okay, I get it. I screwed up. What do I do now?

GEORGE. Crawl on broken glass and apologize. Take whatever she wants to give you. Go to Couples Therapy. Join Sex Addicts Anonymous.

RICHARD. Where the hell do you find that?

GEORGE. I don't know. It's anonymous. Why do you even want to get back with Stephanie if you can't stop going with other women?

RICHARD. I do want to stop, George. I love Stephanie. She's the only real and pure thing in my life. I lose her and I fall into the abyss.

GEORGE. Speaking of which, as soon as I'm done with these e-mails I'm going to go take abyss. *(laughs)* LOL. Laughing my head off.

STEPHANIE. Peg, what went wrong? I did everything he wanted. I gave up my job, I moved out here, I made a beautiful home, met him every night at the door with a drink. For Christ's sake, I was a fantasy wife. And that wasn't enough? I'm a Goddamn idiot!

RICHARD. George, you're a Goddamn idiot. Don't you get it? If I don't clean up my act, I'll wind up like Jack Nicholson in "Carnal Knowledge."

GEORGE. Is that the one with Art Garfunkel?

RICHARD. Ann-Margret's naked through the whole thing and all you remember is Art Garfunkel?

GEORGE. Hey, I have all his albums. Never mind me. You want Stephanie back for good then make sure you get rid of "Bad Skin."

RICHARD. It's not gonna be that easy. I'm afraid to break up with Wanda. She's got a violent temper. That's great in the bedroom, but when she's dressed and standing up screaming in the street it can curl your hair. And on top of that I think she might have crabs.

GEORGE. What a mess. Don't you know the old expression – you lay down with dogs, you wake up with crabs.

RICHARD. That's fleas.

GEORGE. Fleas can get crabs?

RICHARD. How did you pass the Bar?

GEORGE. That wasn't on the test.

GEORGE. Stephanie, are you all right? Richard's a fool. You're an angel and he doesn't deserve you. It breaks my heart that he hurt you. If it makes you feel any better, I just saw him and he's completely miserable. If there's anything I can do, let me know.

WANDA. Richard, you better be laying dead in a hospital somewhere. I can't believe you stood me up. Nobody stands me up. You hear me? Nobody. By the way, I got a ride home from a very nice stockbroker. Young guy. Corvette. Kept looking at my breasts the whole time. And, by the way, he thinks you're an asshole, too.

PEG. George, Stephanie said you e-mailed her a very sweet e-mail. That's really nice of you. P.S. – I hope your man-whore friend's penis gets stuck in an electric pencil sharpener.

GEORGE. Peg, I know. Trust me. I had no idea what was going on.

PEG. I believe you.

(making "jerk-off" motions)

Not!

STEPHANIE. George, thank you so much for your sweet e-mail. You will never know how much it meant to me. At a time when I doubt true gentleman even exist, you give me hope.

RICHARD. Wanda, I'm so sorry about last night. I did try calling you around midnight but didn't want to leave this on a machine. But here goes: my wife knows about us. I would have called earlier, but I was unconscious until around eleven.

WANDA. YEEEESSSSS!!! Richard, can you hear me screaming for joy? I'm actually jumping up and down in my cubicle. You should see me, it's very hot. Linden's looking at me right now. And I'm shaking my ass just to drive him crazy. This is great news. About time you had the balls to finally tell her the truth. How did it happen?

RICHARD. What's the difference? I told her. That's all that matters.

WANDA. Did she cry? Well, what did she expect? Living in her big mansion in Westport with her BMW and her Costco card! You give her all that and she hasn't even had sex with you for the last year.

RICHARD. Yeah, well. Wanda, look, she's very upset. I'm going to need some time here to sort things through.

WANDA. You do what you have to do. I'll see you at my place after work and we can celebrate. Just think. I don't have to feel like a dirty little secret anymore. We can be an actual couple – like Oprah and Gail. And you can finally spend the whole night. Maybe we can do it twice for once and you can take your time 'cause you won't have to rush to catch the last train.

RICHARD. Wanda, I'm afraid I can't meet you tonight. I'm also not coming in to the office today. I need time to think.

WANDA. Think about what? This is what we've dreamed of.

RICHARD. Wanda, this is my marriage we're talking about.

WANDA. Excuse me? This is my life we're talking about!

RICHARD. George, the shit has hit the fan. Wanda thinks just because Stephanie found out about us that now we're gonna be a legitimate couple.

(GEORGE on his BlackBerry.)

GEORGE. You and Stephanie ARE a legitimate couple.

RICHARD. Me and Wanda!

GEORGE. Sorry. Doing two things at once. Hold on.

(SFX: toilet flush)

There. Is it serious with you and Wanda?

RICHARD. No! Are you kidding? You've seen her skin. It was just a fling. A meaningless fling. Look, if anything had the potential to be serious it would have been two years ago with Lisa from accounting.

GEORGE. The blonde with the great legs and the big nostrils? YRAAC!

RICHARD. What's YRAAC?

GEORGE. You-Really-Are-A-Scumbag. Wasn't Lisa engaged? How come I never know about these women?

RICHARD. How do I know? With all due respect you aren't the brightest guy in the world. Remember? You thought it was perfectly normal to come home and find your wife in the basement sitting on the gas man.

GEORGE. Hey, there WAS a funny smell in the house.

WANDA. Richard? Did you get my last e-mail? Where are you? Why aren't you answering me?

RICHARD. Stephanie? Where are you? Why aren't you answering me? I've written at least twenty of these things. Your mother won't tell me where you are. Your sisters won't tell me where you are. Your cell goes straight to voice mail. Please, can't we try to work this out?

WANDA. Dear Richard, I hope you get this. But I'm writing to you here at Art-B-4-Function because this is the address where we had the great cybersex. If this is you, please answer me.

PEG. Oh, I'm here, Wanda. You're a dirty, filthy whore. I will never see you again, you stinking dirty crab-bag! Love, Richard.

WANDA. Nice try, Art! You're real brave – with three floors and the internet between us. If I ever find out who you are, I'll burn your face with cigarettes. You'll have skin like Ray Liotta!

RICHARD. You know what, George? I should live in France. Nobody thinks twice about having a girl on the side over there. You don't have a girl on the side over there, people think you're gay.

STEPHANIE. Peg, I switched rooms. The hotel upgraded me to a suite after I started crying when they asked how long I'd be staying. My eyes are so swollen I look like I have a thyroid problem. I still can't believe it. I mean, my God, why? We were still having sex all the time. We did it on the dining room table just last week.

PEG. Remind me not to eat at your house ever again.

WANDA. Richard, are you OK? Call me. Please. I'm a lot calmer. My brother Polo got me some Xanax. Call me – just so I know you're OK. OK?

GEORGE. Richard? Where are you? Your assistant says you're not in today. I hope you're in therapy with Stephanie and that Wanda's history. Fill me in. P.S. – attached are a few more Hillary Clinton nudes to cheer you up. Happy face.

RICHARD. George, I can't stand staying in this house without Stephanie. It's like a ghost-house. I look in her closet and there's nothing there. I want to go back. Back before I screwed everything up. What have I done?!!

PEG. Stephanie, Richard was just here. He thought I was hiding you in my guest bedroom. He was insane. Screaming. Hyperventilating. His face was all red. I haven't had a guy in my apartment that excited since I was in my early thirties. He's going absolutely crazy. I couldn't be happier.

STEPHANIE. Really? I have fifty-three messages from him on my cell phone and about seventy e-mails I haven't answered. He says he'll do anything to keep us together. Even get counseling. My sister's calling me with the name of a therapist.

PEG. Your sister? The one who's afraid of birds? Are you sure you want to try to save this?

STEPHANIE. I have to. We made a vow. He's my husband and I'm his wife. If I can't make this work then everything I did for the last ten years of my life was nothing but a meaningless joke. I owe him a chance.

PEG. The only thing you owe him is a good swift kick in the balls.

STEPHANIE. I'll try to remember that when I see him tonight for drinks. He just wants a chance to explain. You've never been married, Peg. It's different than dating a guy for two weeks and then breaking up with him when you find out he's gay.

PEG. Thanks.

STEPHANIE. We're meeting at the Nat King Cole Room of the St. Regis. The same place where he proposed. Isn't that sweet?

PEG. YOU ARE AN IDIOT!

GEORGE. Peg, got your e-mail. I agree she's playing with fire. No good can come of this.

PEG. We should do something. Any ideas?

GEORGE. The only idea I can come up with is to smash her in the head with a frying pan and hope that when she wakes up she has no memory of him. JK. Just fooling.

WANDA. George, it's me, Wanda – fourth floor receptionist. I know we haven't been that close at work. But I know you are Richard's best friend so I'm sure you know what's going on. Have you heard from him? I can't reach him. His bitch of an assistant says he'll be away for ten days for personal reasons. Me and my brother Polo drive by his house in Westport every night but everything looks dark and no one answers the bell. I am going crazy. This is really affecting me. I've got blind pimples all over my nose. I want to kill someone. Please help me get in touch with him.

GEORGE. Wanda, I have no idea who you are or what you are talking about. P.S. – here are some pictures of Hillary Clinton that you might find amusing.

(**WANDA** *reacts to the photos.*)

STEPHANIE. Peg, sorry I haven't written lately. Things are getting better. Thank God we're going to therapy. I love it!

RICHARD. George, thank God you've never had to go to therapy. It's brutal. Everything's always my fault. Except for one thing. The fact that Stephanie picked me is apparently HER fault.

STEPHANIE. We're learning so much about each other. I now realize that I did everything for Richard because my mother never did that for my father and I thought that's why he left her. P.S. – and I finally found out why Richard has that irrational fear of anything that foams.

RICHARD. I'm trying my best, George. But I don't know how therapy can help. I don't know why I do the things I do. I really don't. I love Stephanie. I do. But I also love spaghetti. I just don't want to eat it for the rest of my life. Not that I don't love spaghetti. I do. But sometimes you want to eat it off a plate. And sometimes you want to eat it out of a bowl. And sometimes you want to eat it off the stomach of a 23 year-old Latin girl.

GEORGE. You lost me. Who is the spaghetti? Stephanie? Or the other one? You know, I ate food off a girl's stomach once. My fork got stuck in her belly button ring and…let's just say I won't be doing that again anytime soon. Thanks a lot. Now I'm hungry.

STEPHANIE. Peg. Therapy is so intense. Our therapist Judith makes Richard and me explore what attracted us to each other in the first place. And why I gave up so much of myself. And why Richard is so full of excuses. She's like a pit bull. She calls him on every stupid thing he says.

RICHARD. In today's session I tried to explain that this cheating stuff is actually science's fault. That way back in cavemen days, man was only supposed to live until he was thirty. So by the time he got bored with his wife he was, you know, dead. But this therapist woman didn't buy it. Told me I was full of shit. I think that's because she's way over thirty and obviously divorced. (no ring) Impartial, my ass.

PEG. FYI. I hit a new low last night. I'm out on a blind date only to discover he's Bozo the Clown's son. Not even the original Bozo. The one that went to supermarket openings. And I swear to God – his nose was big and red and he had a polka-dot shirt on! I'm so done! Match-dot-com can go-fuck-itself-dot-com.

RICHARD. This week the therapist made me give Stephanie access to my computer and cell phone codes. To build trust. I don't know about trust but Stephanie is having a field day with the messages and e-mails that Wanda keeps leaving.

WANDA. Richard, you bastard. I can't believe you're cutting me out of your life. Like I'm some little whore. Well, I'm not a whore!

RICHARD. But you'd be proud of me, George. I am being good and not having any contact with her.

GEORGE. Good. Stay away from her. She's nuts.

WANDA. Richard, how can you ignore me like this? You're the one who said you couldn't live without me after I blew you in the men's room on bobblehead nighta at CitiField Stadium.

STEPHANIE. You won't believe the e-mails that tramp sends. I don't know how Richard could ever touch her. She's so vulgar and common. I bet you she uses the bathroom at Port Authority. Richard made me go to the doctor because he thinks she might have crabs.

(**PEG** *reacts.*)

STEPHANIE. And get this. This is not the first married man she's dated. She dated her Uncle Diego and HE was married.

RICHARD. Hey George, the Mets lost. You owe me fifty bucks. So anyway, this therapist – her name is Judith – blames this cheating stuff on my mother. Yeah. Like my mother told Wanda to ask me to lunch that first time and put her foot in my crotch. I don't think so. But on a good note, I have to say the stress has made Stephanie lose so much weight she's had to buy all new clothes. She looks really hot. So you can't say nothing good has come out of this affair.

PEG. Stephanie, I know you really want this to work out. But wouldn't it just be easier to tie a cement bag around your ankle and drag that around for the rest of your life? Do you really trust him?

STEPHANIE. I'm learning to. This is a marriage. For better or worse. He's my husband. Despite the horrible things you said about him.

(**PEG** *reacts.*)

GEORGE. Peg, you can't win. If she stays with him she's going to remember all the rotten things you said about him. And if she breaks up with him, she'll blame you for starting it. You should have said nothing. That's what I did, which is why I come off smelling like a rose.

PEG. Dear Wanda, your Uncle Diego called. He has crabs, too.

WANDA. Who the hell told you that? He wasn't my real uncle, you son of a bitch! I'll shove sticks in your eyes so hard YOUR uncle will go blind!!

RICHARD. Stephanie, I know Judith says we shouldn't talk outside of therapy but I want you to know how much I love you for giving me another chance. I can't say I love going there, but I'll do whatever it takes. The best part is I get to see you twice a week.

STEPHANIE. Richard, I know it can't be easy to hear how damaging it was that you took a bath with your mother until you were eleven. But therapy is the only chance we have. I better go. I don't want to jinx anything. See you in therapy. Love, your hopefully not ex-wife.

RICHARD. George, I think your obsession with nude shots of Hillary Clinton is getting out of control. Don't you think it's time you started dating? I know a fourth floor receptionist who's free.

GEORGE. Thanks for the disgusting offer. I would never date anyone you slept with. How's the therapy going?

RICHARD. It's been a wild two months. Stephanie still hasn't moved back in. But she did agree to have drinks with me last night. I tried to get her loaded on mojitos but she still wouldn't come home.

GEORGE. I'm glad for you, buddy. Welcome back from the Dark Side. Stephanie is the greatest thing that ever happened to you. Do you remember what you told me the first time you went out with her?

RICHARD. "Fifty bucks the carpet doesn't match the drapes."

GEORGE. You said "This is the one. The one worth giving up all other women." And she still is. Remember that. Oh. Thought you'd like to know, my assistant says Wanda looks terrible these days. She's breaking out, not washing her hair, and I don't know what the hell is going on with her nose. There's stuff growing on there that looks like potato eyes. Boy, when you break a heart you really break a heart.

PEG. Dear Wanda, all the girls at the office say you look like shit. That's because you are shit. Why don't you eat yourself and die.

WANDA. I find out who the hell you are, Art, I'll pepper spray your mouth and duct tape your lips shut!

GEORGE. Peg, your worst fear has come true.

PEG. They outlawed trans-fats?

GEORGE. Stephanie and Richard are back together. I called the house early this morning and Stephanie answered the phone. She must have spent the night. She had an after-sex voice.

PEG. "After-sex voice?"

GEORGE. You know, a husky dreamy voice. Like Kathleen Turner without the fake accent.

PEG. You're creeping me out. First those naked Hillary Clinton photos and now this.

GEORGE. Didn't you think those photos were funny?

PEG. No! Why would I think naked pictures of Hillary Clinton are funny?

GEORGE. Look how big I made her nipples. LOL. Laughing very loud.

PEG. You need to date. Badly.

GEORGE. I know. I know. I've had tickets to "The Lion King" for three months and kept thinking I'd meet someone by now. But time flew by, it's this Friday and I'm still going alone. How sad is that?

PEG. I'm free Friday.

(**GEORGE** *stares at the screen.*)

PEG. George, are you there?

(**GEORGE** *stares at the screen.*)

PEG. George?

GEORGE. To Whom It May Concern, I'm out of the office for the day. Please contact my assistant if this is an emergency.

PEG. Asshole!

STEPHANIE. Peg, just wanted you to know that Richard and I are officially going to give it another try. I know you didn't want this, but I love him. And he loves me. And it's going to be different this time. My eyes are wide open now. I might even go back to work. You'll see. My whole life isn't going to just be about him. It's all good. And I hope you can be happy for us.

(**PEG** *debates what to write back. Chooses not to write anything.*)

GEORGE. Stephanie, I hear therapy is going well. Richard is like a man with a mission. And the mission is you. Anyway, your friend Peg kind of asked me out and I got scared and kind of blew her off and then she kind of called me an asshole. What do I do?

STEPHANIE. Wow, I didn't know you guys talked. Peg is a great girl and I feel kind of bad because she was so there for me when I found out about Richard and the slut. And now that we are working it out we don't talk as much. I think you should just tell her the truth and apologize. Believe me, the truth is ALWAYS better. And she really is a great girl.

GEORGE. Is she cute?

STEPHANIE. She's an architect.

GEORGE. *(impressed)* Really?

WANDA. Richard? Are you there?

(**RICHARD** *stares at the screen, fights the urge to write back.*)

GEORGE. Richard. Just writing to tell you how proud I am of you. You're really doing it. Be good to Stephanie. She deserves it.

RICHARD. Thanks, George. I can't tell you how good it is to be back with Stephanie.

GEORGE. Why not?

RICHARD. Why not what?

GEORGE. Why can't you tell me how good it is?

RICHARD. That's an expression. That's the problem with e-mails. You can't hear inflection. I was just using an expression.

GEORGE. What expression?

RICHARD. "I can't tell you."

(GEORGE reacts.)

GEORGE. Why not?

RICHARD. No. That's it – "I can't tell you."

GEORGE. What do you mean, "that's it?"

RICHARD. That's it: "I can't tell you."

GEORGE. What did I do?

RICHARD. Nothing. That's it.

GEORGE. What's it?

RICHARD. "I can't tell you."

GEORGE. Why not?

RICHARD. That's the expression.

GEORGE. What is?

RICHARD. "I can't tell you."

GEORGE. Why not?

RICHARD. No, that's it. "I can't tell you."

GEORGE. What's it?

RICHARD. "I can't tell you."

GEORGE. Well, screw you then.

RICHARD. No. You're not understanding me. The sentence is: "I can't tell you how good it is." The expression: "I – CAN'T – TELL – YOU.

GEORGE. FINE – THEN – SHOVE – IT – UP – YOUR – ASS. Here's an expression for you: ! $ # % & X $!!

RICHARD. What is that supposed to mean?

GEORGE. *(smug)* I can't tell you!

(**GEORGE** *reacts triumphantly.*)

WANDA. Richard, I can't stand this. I ride that elevator twenty-five times a day hoping I'll see you. And when I do you won't even look at me. What do I have to do to get you to talk to me? Throw myself on the hood of your car in your driveway? I'll do it. You're breaking my heart. I miss you, my dirty little janitor.

(**RICHARD** *hesitates, several times. Then gives in and starts typing.*)

RICHARD. Wanda. Because of what happened before, I am writing this from my corporate e-mail. I don't know what to say. I miss you, too. But I'm afraid this is how things are.

WANDA. Fine. You'll see. You don't belong with her. I only hope I'll still be here when you wake up and realize I'm the one that you want. X. X. X. O. O. O. V.

(**RICHARD** *thinks.*)

RICHARD. I know Xs are kisses and Os are hugs, but what's a "V"?

WANDA. That's me laying on my back with my legs in the air.

(**RICHARD** *reacts, intrigued at the thought.*)

(lights down)

(lights up on **RICHARD***)*

RICHARD. George, I got a second cell phone. Here's the number.

GEORGE. Why a second cell phone?

RICHARD. Why all the questions? Get off my back.

GEORGE. Peg, I had a great time with you the other night. Sorry I didn't recognize you right away in the bar. But with that suit, from the back I thought you were a business man.

PEG. George, I had a very nice time, too. The play was great. And I don't think you're less of a man. Simba seeing his Dad's ghost made me tear up, too. Can't believe we saw Hillary Clinton there.

GEORGE. Pig, I know. I can't stop laughing about seeing her there.

PEG. That's Peg.

GEORGE. What's Peg?

PEG. My name. You addressed me in the last e-mail as "pig."

GEORGE. Sorry. Typing fast. Spell-check doesn't catch those. I had a great time with you and would love to see you again. Engorged.

PEG. What?

GEORGE. I meant to sign that, "George."

STEPHANIE. Peg, it's been two weeks. But time flies when you're saving a marriage. Therapy's going great! I know what you think of Richard but he's been fantastic. He sends me flowers every day. And he even wrote me a poem.

PEG. God help me.

STEPHANIE. It's called 'Ode to You.' By Richard Nathan Winters. "I can't believe I almost lost thee. I shudder to think what it almost cost me"…

PEG. Jesus Christ.

STEPHANIE. "I vow to be true, and stray I will never. It's Stephanie and Richard for ever and ever."

(**PEG** *sticks her finger down her throat.*)

STEPHANIE. He's putting it to music tonight at a karaoke bar! I guess you were wrong about him.

GEORGE. Stephanie. You were right about Peg. She's a very special girl. And we had a marvelous time. Thanks for pushing me.

STEPHANIE. Peg, I haven't heard back from you. I know you're still upset about Richard. I understand. But I want you to know I'm so happy for you and George. You are two of the nicest people I know and are so perfect for each other. I can't wait to tell Richard.

RICHARD. George, you slimy traitor. I just found out about you and that big lump of shit. Like a knife in my back, pal. A big fat butter knife. That dump truck is the one who ruined my life.

GEORGE. Thanks for being happy for me.

RICHARD. I'm just happy she hasn't crushed you to death yet. Are you stupid? You have some nerve. A big Goddamn nerve. What kind of a friend are you? And how can you sleep with her? She has a beard.

GEORGE. One hair! And Richard, I must ask you to stop besmirching Peg. You may think her life is a bed of roses, but it's snot.

RICHARD. Her life is "snot?"

GEORGE. "Not!" I hit an extra "s."

RICHARD. Well, if anyone's going to have an extra "s," it's Peg.

GEORGE. Listen. Instead of insulting Peg, you should be thanking her. If it wasn't for Peg you would still be sneaking around screwing Wanda any time you wanted and Stephanie wouldn't know a thing...

(**RICHARD** *reacts, as if to say "no kidding."*)

GEORGE. ...Don't you see? This thing was a land mine waiting to explode. If you'd kept seeing that gold-digger, you would've lost Stephanie forever, not to mention your house and your money. And you could forget about ever being made a partner. Wanda's bad news. Even the paralegals know she has crabs.

RICHARD. You're right. You're right. Too bad I can't legally fire her.

GEORGE. Not unless she starts embezzling.

(**RICHARD** *reacts.*)

WANDA. Hi, Lover. What a night. You were unbelievable. How can one man pack so much passion into so little time? That was so exciting. And so hot. There's nothing like us. Nothing. We were so meant to be. How's next Thursday, Loverman?

(RICHARD reacts.)

STEPHANIE. Richard, had lunch with your mother today. She got a little angry when I told her Judith said your problems were all her fault. She said that's a crock. She took baths with her brother until she was fourteen and she turned out fine, Goddammit.

WANDA. Richard? It's been two days. Why aren't you answering me? Are we still on for Thursday or not?

(RICHARD reacts.)

GEORGE. Richard, wild day here at the office. Guess you heard. Wanda's been fired. They found office supplies in her bag. Tons of stuff. It was all crammed in there and sitting right on top of her desk in plain sight. She denied all knowledge of it, of course, but no one cares. That security guy Linden escorted her from the building and she was screaming like a drunken Red Sox fan. Looks like you're off the hook. She's gone!

WANDA. Richard? I don't know what happened today. I don't understand it. I went to the ladies room and when I came back, my pocketbook was on top of my desk stuffed with staplers, law books, a telephone, and a fax machine. And next thing I know that ass-wipe Linden threw me out of the building like I was some sort of homeless person trying to use the bathroom. Richard, please. Is there anything you can do?

(RICHARD stares at the screen.)

RICHARD. Stephanie, good news. I had Wanda officially fired today. Even though you've been great about it, I knew it bothered you that she was still here. And nobody bothers my girl.

STEPHANIE. Richard, I can't tell you how much that means to me.

WANDA. Richard? Did you get my last e-mail? Why aren't you answering your phone? Don't do this to me again. I don't even know how I'm going to pay my rent.

(RICHARD stares at the screen.)

WANDA. Dear Art, please have Richard call me. Wanda.

PEG. Dear Wanda, sure, I'll have Richard call you. When pigs fly. And I don't think you're flying anytime soon, pig.

(PEG laughs at herself.)

PEG. High five!

(PEG high-fives herself. WANDA reacts.)

RICHARD. Hi, Stephanie, it's me, your very happy husband. I was just sitting here thinking how I feel closer to you than ever before. I'm a new man. And it's all because you saved me. Saved me from myself.

STEPHANIE. I feel the same way. I love you so much. I almost feel like calling that slut Wanda and telling her she can try all she wants but she will never break us up.

RICHARD. Well, let's not do that. And you don't have to worry about Wanda ever again. She's gone for good.

WANDA. Richard, we need to talk.

(RICHARD stares at the screen.)

RICHARD. Steph, we should go somewhere great. Just you and me. How about Little Dix Bay? Or Tortola? I'll get us a romantic cabin on the beach and we can make love in the surf all day and under the stars all night.

WANDA. Richard, we really need to talk.

(RICHARD stares at the screen.)

PEG. George, last weekend was so amazing. Five times in one night. You're pretty special, Tater Tot. I can't believe we are actually, like, boyfriend and girlfriend now. Do people our age still say that?

GEORGE. Peg, after last weekend you better believe it, Girlfriend. Yowza! Yeah, it does feel weird. I went from a lousy marriage, to a pathetic divorced loser and now I've got you. Pretty cool, huh? Happy face.

STEPHANIE. Peg, we just got back from a week in Tortola. I've never been happier. And I'm tan. All over. We almost did it twice in one day, too, but Richard got sunburned on his you know what. Spent the rest of the day with it stuck inside a bottle of aloe vera. Oh, well. It's always something. But life is great. My only hope is that you and George are as happy as we are.

PEG. We are. For the first time in my life I am truly happy. And I have you to thank.

STEPHANIE. Peg, that's great. I bet you two look so cute together.

PEG. We do! We can even share pants.

STEPHANIE. That's fantastic. How about we double date next week?

PEG. Sorry, Stephanie. I'm busy that night.

STEPHANIE. I didn't pick a night.

PEG. Oh.

WANDA. Richard, I didn't want to say this in an e-mail but you won't Goddamn answer me. I'm pregnant.

*(**RICHARD** chokes on his coffee.)*

STEPHANIE. Richard, we're all set for next Friday. You, me, George and Peg. Should be fun.

WANDA. Richard? Are you there?

STEPHANIE. Richard? Are you there?

RICHARD. George! Are you there? She's pregnant!

*(**GEORGE** writes his answers on a BlackBerry.)*

GEORGE. Stephanie? That's fantastic! I Tortola ya to go to the Bahamas.

RICHARD. Not Stephanie. Wanda! She said she couldn't get pregnant.

GEORGE. Who, Stephanie?

RICHARD. Wanda! Follow along.

GEORGE. Sorry. I'm in the middle of a deposition. Typing this on the sly. Maybe she's lying. She slept with a married man. You can't trust a woman like that.

RICHARD. I don't know. She's never lied to me before. She said I was the best she ever had, and I'm sure THAT's true. God, what if she is pregnant? She did look a little chubby the last time I saw her.

GEORGE. That means nothing. I'm a little chubby. And I'm completely barren. What did you say to her when she told you?

RICHARD. I never answered her.

GEORGE. Are you an idiot? Don't get her mad. She'll call Stephanie! Write her back now and tell her how excited you are. If you hurt that girl again I'll kill you.

RICHARD. Wanda?

GEORGE. Stephanie!

RICHARD. Why are you always so concerned about Stephanie? I thought you were MY friend.

GEORGE. Just do it! Tell Wanda you think it's exciting and you want to meet at the bar at the top of the Peninsula Hotel!

RICHARD. Really?

GEORGE. Yes! Then buy her champagne, walk her to the balcony, make a toast, and as she takes a sip, slam her in the small of the back and send her plummeting twenty-three floors to her death.

(**GEORGE** *can't stop laughing.*)

RICHARD. Asshole!

GEORGE. Gotta go. A whole conference room of people are staring at me.

RICHARD. Wanda, sorry I didn't answer you before. But this came as a bit of a shock. I thought you said you couldn't get pregnant.

WANDA. I couldn't. This must be a sign from God. Like in that movie "Miracle on 34th Street."

RICHARD. We have to talk.

WANDA. I know. We got a lot to plan. Come to my apartment after work. I'll tell my brother Polo to go bowling so we can be alone.

RICHARD. Christ.

WANDA. And, hey, since you're still in the office, bring the jump rope and the janitor bucket.

RICHARD. What do I do? What do I do? And she's Catholic.

STEPHANIE. Richard, hi. It's me. I made 7:00 reservations at the Riverside. I got our favorite table, the corner booth.

RICHARD. Shit.

(in e-mail)

Oh, Steph. I'm sorry. Something just came up.

(to himself)

Goddammit.

(in e-mail)

Probably won't be home 'til the middle of the night.

(to himself)

Shit.

(in e-mail)

I'll make it up to you tomorrow.

(to himself)

Goddammit.

(in e-mail)

Dreaming about our booth. Love, me. Shit Goddammit.

*(**STEPHANIE** reacts.)*

STEPHANIE. Really. Oh, well, honey. That sounds bad. Don't worry, I'll make the reservation for tomorrow. Dreaming about our booth, too, shit goddammit.

(**RICHARD** *reacts.*)

PEG. George, I hope you are hungry because I am making a fantastic steak and lobster dinner for you. With a fabulous Pinot Noir and homemade creme brulee for dessert.

GEORGE. Don't forget to wear that little apron I like and I'll bring my "Lion King" soundtrack. Can you feel the love tonight? George.

PEG. Happy face.

GEORGE. Happy face.

STEPHANIE. George, it's me – Stephanie. Is Richard still in his office? He's not answering his cell.

GEORGE. Which one?

(**STEPHANIE** *reacts.*)

STEPHANIE. "Which one?"

(*to* **GEORGE**)

Uh...Both of them.

GEORGE. He's gone. He left over an hour ago. (*lying very poorly*) Either he's been in a horrible bus accident or else he's rushing home to you.

STEPHANIE. Okay, thanks.

(*to herself*)

Bus accident...

(*types*)

Dear Peg, how do I get into someone's corporate e-mail?

PEG. I'll refrain from asking whose. But if you give me Richard's social security number and birth date I think I can figure it out. But make it quick, I'm in the middle of something.

STEPHANIE. Here you go.

GEORGE. Richard? Where are you? Stephanie's looking for you. I've called both cell phones and searched the whole building. No one knows where you are. The little janitor lady told me to look in the men's room on the fourth floor but you weren't there either. Man, that place smells like Fritos. Hope everything's all right.

PEG. Stephanie, there you are. You're in. Gotta go.

(STEPHANIE types in some keystrokes, reads, and sits back.)

STEPHANIE. You bastard.

(lights down)

(lights up on RICHARD)

(He types on a BlackBerry.)

RICHARD. Stephanie, where the heck are you? I can't get in the house. Something is wrong with all the locks. And why aren't you answering your cell? I'm in the car freezing my ass off, writing on my BlackBerry, wondering if I should call the police.

PEG. George, where are you? Are you okay? I've tried reaching you everywhere. The steak is burned and I ate all the lobster, plus a half bucket of clams. Please call me.

WANDA. Richard, I know we didn't get to say much tonight, you animal, you. But I know what you wanted to say. And from the way my body responded, you know my answer. Love, the future Mrs. Richard Nathan Winters.

RICHARD. Call me!

PEG. Call me!

WANDA. Call me.

(RICHARD types on his BlackBerry.)

RICHARD. George, Goddammit. I've been ringing your doorbell for an hour. I know you're in there. I can hear the "Lion King" playing. I need your help. I can't find Stephanie. This thing with Wanda is out of control. Why aren't you answering your phone?

(PEG is on her BlackBerry.)

PEG. George, what is happening? I drove past your apartment and saw Richard standing in your lobby. I knew this had something to do with that slime ball. What did pig-face do now? It's not your job to clean up after him. I'm at the McDonalds on Park and 28th.

WANDA. Richard? I'm so excited I can't sleep. I'm lying here picturing how to redecorate your…I mean, our… house in Westport. I think we should put in a couple of fountains and a statue of a little jockey so people think we have servants…

PEG. George? Where the hell are you?

STEPHANIE. George, sorry I'm doing this in an e-mail. I didn't want to wake you. God I was hysterical tonight. I didn't know who to turn to. Thank you for being there for me. Sorry about the spilled wine.

GEORGE. Think nothing of it. Some things are worth a ruined carpet. At least after all the hell you've been through now there is a light at the end of the tunnel.

STEPHANIE. What light, George? Things are worse now. We slept together! Not once, not twice, but six and a half times!

GEORGE. Sorry about that last one, when I heard my mother's voice on the answering machine I sort of lost my concentration.

WANDA. …This is so exciting. I never lived in a house before. You know what I'm gonna do? I'm going to lord it all over everyone! I'm gonna mow our lawn in a negligee and high heels like Eva Longoria!

STEPHANIE. Oh God, George, what are we going to do? I mean, what were we thinking?

GEORGE. I know what I was thinking.

STEPHANIE. George, what we did tonight can never happen again.

GEORGE. What!? *(holding back tears)* Hey, I know that. Don't you think I know that? Everyone knows guys like me never get girls like you.

STEPHANIE. We can never tell anyone.

GEORGE. You're right. Except, of course, for Peg. I guess I should just tell her the truth.

STEPHANIE. No!!

GEORGE. ...I suppose if she really loves me she will understand.

RICHARD. Stephanie, I'm getting a coffee at a McDonald's on Park and 28th. Your friend Peg is sleeping three tables away with her head on a filet of fish sandwich. What the hell is going on? I'll try calling you again.

STEPHANIE. George, please don't tell her it was me! I feel bad enough! I feel like Richard. I'm worse than Richard, because you and Peg are my friends.

GEORGE. Stephanie, you left your cell phone here. It's ringing under the bed. Omigod! It's Richard calling. Should I answer it? No! I'm not answering it.

RICHARD. George, things didn't go exactly as planned with Wanda. When I arrived at her house she was naked and had a baby name book. So what else could I do? We made love while she called out different baby names. P.S. – She likes Usher, Owen and Keanu. And Jesus.

WANDA. ...And we'll have to get all new furniture, too. 'Cause, pardon me, I'm not putting my ass on anything she ever touched. Except, of course, for your face.

GEORGE. Stephanie, you comparing yourself to Richard broke my heart. You are nothing like Richard. You are an angel. Last night might have been wrong but it was like a dream to me. One I will always cherish.

STEPHANIE. Oh, George, that is the sweetest thing anyone has ever said to me. I don't know if I will ever get past last night. What kind of a person am I? It was so wrong.

GEORGE. *(holding back tears)* Of course. But I want you to know those six and a half times will live in my heart forever.

PEG. George, I'm home now. They made me leave the McDonald's. Apparently no matter how much you order you can't fall asleep in there. Please call me. Or come here. Or write me.

*(**RICHARD** is back on his laptop.)*

RICHARD. Stephanie, where the hell are you? I'm back at the office sleeping on a couch. This is like an episode of "The Twilight Zone" where I don't live in our house anymore.

STEPHANIE. You don't live in our house anymore, Richard. The locks are changed. And it's none of your Goddamn business where I was last night. But I know where you were. And who you were with. Congratulations on the baby. Is this your first? I mean, there have been so many women over the last ten years. Nice corporate e-mails. See attached.

(**RICHARD** *reacts.*)

RICHARD. Ahhhh! Ahhhhhh!

STEPHANIE. P.S. – You've gotten your last XX OO from this wife. And never again will you see my "V."

GEORGE. Peg, I am so, so, sorry about last night. Something happened and I need to talk to you as soon as possible. Can you meet me at my apartment? I can be there by noon. Please say you'll be there.

RICHARD. OK, OK, Stephanie. I admit it. Jesus, I told you I had a problem. Ask Judith. In therapy last week I hit on her when you went to get your coat. This is all my mother's fault, remember? It's an illness. Like Lupus. I can't stop. In fact, I'm winking at the midget janitor lady as I'm writing this. But you are the only one I love. I swear on your mother's life. I don't even know why I went with Wanda. She's crazy. I don't even know if this kid is mine. She's a pathological liar. Not to mention the whole skin thing. Plus her feet are too big for her body. And the worst of it is, quite frankly, sometimes she smells.

STEPHANIE. Dear Wanda. Please enjoy this forward from Richard. Signed, Richard's ex-wife.

(**WANDA** *reacts.*)

WANDA. Richard, you shrimp-dicked bastard. So I have big feet and smell, huh?

RICHARD. That wasn't written by me. There's a guy down the hall…Hal Something…HE thinks you have big feet and smell. He's a jerk.

WANDA. You're the jerk. A big-footed smelly can-only-do-it-one-time-a-night jerk. I hate you. I'll choke you so hard with piano wire your head will slice off like pepperoni.

WANDA. Dear Stephanie, be nasty if you want but your marriage went to shit because your husband couldn't keep his hands off me, you frigid bitch. P.S. I don't smell.

STEPHANIE. Wanda, don't flatter yourself. You're not the first and you won't be the last. In fact, here's a list.

(**WANDA** *reacts.*)

STEPHANIE. You should know a few, considering you worked with half of them. And about your last comment? Don't be too sure. There's a smell that comes through my computer every time you write to me.

STEPHANIE. To all clients of Richard Nathan Winters, junior partner for Ryan, Murphy and Kubel, thought you'd like to see what you paid for when invoiced for time my husband allegedly spent at the St. Regis doing legal work on your behalf. Attach: Photo file. cc: Entire client address book. Send.

(**RICHARD** *and* **GEORGE** *gasp.*)

RICHARD. Mother of God, what are you doing, Stephanie? This is serious shit. Doesn't ten years together count for anything?

STEPHANIE. Yes. Half the house, half your stocks, half your pension, and a nice fat alimony check.

PEG. George, don't bother leaving the office. I got to your apartment early with a picnic lunch that is now all over your walls. Next time you invite your girlfriend over, make sure you don't leave your computer on with e-mails from your one-night stand on the desk top. Good thing you have a dream to cherish, because you no longer have me. Can you feel the hate tonight?

(GEORGE reacts.)

RICHARD. George…

GEORGE. Aah!

RICHARD. …where the hell are you? I need to talk to you. The shit has really hit the fan.

GEORGE. I hear ya, buddy.

GEORGE. Peg, please answer the phone. Don't make me do this in an e-mail. You're worth more than that. We're worth more than that. Please talk to me. Or let me come over. I am so sorry. You will never know how sorry. It was a mistake. Everybody makes a mistake.

PEG. Yes, and mine was going to see the "Lion King" with someone low enough to screw my best friend. SIX AND A HALF TIMES! I hate you.

STEPHANIE. Dear Messrs. Ryan, Murphy & Kubel. Thought you'd like to know how your junior partner Richard Nathan Winters spends his time – with smelly fax machine-stealing former-receptionists. Please enjoy the following photos.

RICHARD/GEORGE. Ah!/Oh!

RICHARD/GEORGE. Ooh!/Ah!

RICHARD/GEORGE. God!/Yes!

GEORGE. That's a keeper!

(Everyone reacts.)

STEPHANIE. George, you just replied to "all."

GEORGE. Whoops.

(types)

To All. That last e-mail was a joke. I don't normally send those but it was really funny.

RICHARD. Stephanie. What did you do to me? I'm begging you. Stop! What about all our beautiful memories?

STEPHANIE. Don't worry, Richard. I'll always have my memories. Every time I see a pregnant whore, I'll think of you.

RICHARD. How can this get any worse?

PEG. Richard, it gives me great pleasure to tell you that your best friend George is porking your wife. L.M.F.A.O. Laughing my fat ass off.

(**RICHARD** *gasps.*)

RICHARD. *(to himself)* No!!!! You son of a bitch.

(*to* **GEORGE**)

George! You son of a bitch!

(**GEORGE** *gasps.*)

GEORGE. Stephanie, Omigod, he knows!

(**STEPHANIE** *gasps, then:*)

STEPHANIE. Who knows?

GEORGE. Richard knows!

(**STEPHANIE** *gasps.*)

STEPHANIE. How do you know he knows?

GEORGE. Actually, I don't know he knows. I just know.

STEPHANIE. What?

RICHARD. George, I know!

(**GEORGE** *gasps.*)

GEORGE. Stephanie, now I know he knows.

STEPHANIE. No!

GEORGE. Richard. It was an accident, I tell you. An accident!

RICHARD. It HAD to be an accident! How else could you sleep with a pretty girl?

(**GEORGE** *gasps in resentment.*)

STEPHANIE. George, why did you tell him?

RICHARD. Stephanie, how dare you sleep with George! Why didn't you just run me over with your car?!

STEPHANIE. I'll be happy to. Wait in the middle of the road and I'll be right over. How does it feel picturing ME naked with someone else?!

GEORGE. Stephanie, I didn't tell him. Peg must have told him. By the way, your phone's ringing again.

PEG. Stephanie, you little chicken shit. Too afraid to answer your Goddamn phone? I swear to Christ I will kill both of you.

STEPHANIE. I'm so sorry, Peg, I feel sick about this.

(**RICHARD** *on his BlackBerry.*)

RICHARD. George, stay where you are. I'm coming to kill you. Prepare to die! And this time when I ring the bell, answer the Goddamn door.

PEG. Not as sick as I feel. He was MY boyfriend, you skinny-assed slut.

GEORGE. Help. He's coming to get me!

STEPHANIE. Peg, I swear it was a mistake!

PEG. Mistake, my fat ass! Six and a half times, you botoxed bitch!

GEORGE. Dear Richard, I'm not in right now. I've left town suddenly. For further assistance please e-mail my ass.

(**RICHARD** *reacts.*)

GEORGE. I meant to write "Assistant." But I'm STILL out of town!

RICHARD. How could you go with him? You belong to me! I can't live without you!

STEPHANIE. Then die!

PEG. Wanda, for your information, Richard's wife is a slut, too. She did it six and a half times last night with his best friend. So there, you pocked-marked low-life.

WANDA. Six and a half times?

GEORGE. Omigod. Somebody's at my door.

WANDA. Richard, I want your stuff out of my apartment! I'll never marry you now!

GEORGE. All clear. Paper boy.

RICHARD. I was never going to marry you, you stupid idiot!

(**WANDA** *gasps.*)

WANDA. Yeah? Well, I'm not even pregnant! Who's the stupid idiot now!?

(**RICHARD** *gasps.*)

STEPHANIE. Maybe I'm pregnant. We did it six and a half times!

(**RICHARD** *gasps.*)

RICHARD. George, I'm speeding down Lexington right now! You have about ten minutes left to live.

GEORGE. Ah! Stephanie, lak jimmit go pop a hargtooth flan.

STEPHANIE. What? George, I have no idea what you wrote to me.

GEORGE. Sorry. I'm under the bed and I can't see the keyboard.

(**GEORGE** *pulls out a flashlight and shines it on his keyboard as he writes.*)

GEORGE. Richard, you want to get mad at someone, get mad at yourself. Your degenerate behavior caused all of this.

(**RICHARD** *is on his BlackBerry.*)

RICHARD. Don't you blame me, you son of a bitch!

STEPHANIE. I hate you, Richard. You son of a bitch!

PEG. You're just like him, you son of a bitch!

GEORGE. You're the son of a bitch!

WANDA. Why am I a son of a bitch?

GEORGE. Sorry. Wrong address. It's still a little dark down here.

(*to* **RICHARD**)

Richard, YOU'RE the son of a bitch.

(**RICHARD** *on his BlackBerry.*)

RICHARD. I hate your fleshy Irish face, George! And I can't tell you how much I'm going to enjoy beating your fleshy Irish face into a bloody Irish pulp.

GEORGE. Good, because I don't want to hear how much!

RICHARD. That's the expression again, you retarded moron!

GEORGE. I still don't get it.

RICHARD. Oh, you'll get it now because I'm driving up your block and I'm gonna –

(**RICHARD** *screams.*)

(*a black out*)

(*a beat*)

(*lights up on* **GEORGE**)

GEORGE. Peg, I guess you heard about Richard's car accident. Can't believe he slammed into the lobby of my building. Amazing he's still alive. Which is more than I can say for poor old Mrs. Kirschenbaum. What a bad time for her to be checking her mail. Anyway, I know you don't want to see me anymore. And I can't say I blame you, but…I just wanted to write and tell you that the six weeks we spent together were some of the best meals of my life. P.S. – you can keep the pants I lent you. Sad face. Goodbye, Peg.

(*Lights out on* **GEORGE**.)

WANDA. Dear Art. It's me, Wanda. Hard to believe I wasted a year of my life and lost my job over that shit-sack. You've always been pretty direct. So tell me. Why did I go with him? Why do I always go after unavailable men? Is there something wrong with me?

PEG. Wanda, it's very simple. Most men are scum. No matter how great you think they are, it always ends the same way. Either they turn out to be gay or they pork your best friend. Be glad you're done with that petrified piece of rat shit. You're a beautiful girl. Step back, appreciate yourself, and find someone that you deserve.

WANDA. You're right. I do deserve better. Art, I don't want you to think I'm an easy lay or anything…but…are YOU seeing anyone?

(**PEG** *reacts. Thinks. Then:*)

PEG. No…No, I'm not.

(**WANDA** *reacts with hopeful glee.*)

(*lights out on* **WANDA**)

PEG. Stephanie, I know it's been a while. But I wanted to write and tell you, I'm no longer mad at you. In fact, I want to thank you. This past year was a big wake up call for me. You might say this dog has been barking up the wrong tree. I'll explain more when I see you. I'm leaving next week on a Rosie O'Donnell Cruise. When I get back we should have lunch. I know this great little place we can meet. It's called She-Bang.

RICHARD. Stephanie, are you there? It's been a long time since the accident. Maybe you didn't know, but I lived. Or maybe you came to see me when I was in the coma and they forgot to tell me. Anyway, they're treating me well in rehab. And I haven't flirted with anyone. That must mean I'm improving, right? Or maybe it's just because I no longer have a penis. Yes, you heard that right. I'm suing those "Jaws of Life" people.

(*Lights out on* **RICHARD**.)

STEPHANIE. Richard, wanted you to know I shipped the last of your boxes to your mother's house. It's nice that she's there to take care of you. At least she has plenty of experience giving you baths. And I never thought I'd say this to you, but thank you. If it weren't for the computer you gave me and the e-mails you sent, I wouldn't have found myself. I wouldn't have found true love and happiness with George. And he and I wouldn't be the proud parents of our beautiful baby girl. PS – We named her Hillary.

(*blackout*)

(*For CURTAIN CALL, we hear Elton John singing "Can You hear the Love Tonight?" from the "Lion King."**)

(*Cell phone photos of the actors from the play's various embarrassing off-stage scenes flash behind them on the computer screen. We see Wanda taking her panties off in the St. Regis bar; George with an obviously fake semi-nude Hillary Clinton; Richard in a clinch with a naked Wanda in the elevator; Stephanie's wedding photo looking blissfully happy – with Richard's face cut out of the photo.)*

(As the lights dim from the company bow...)

COMPUTER VOICE. *(V.O.) (signing off)* Good-bye!

---

*See Music Use Note on page 3.

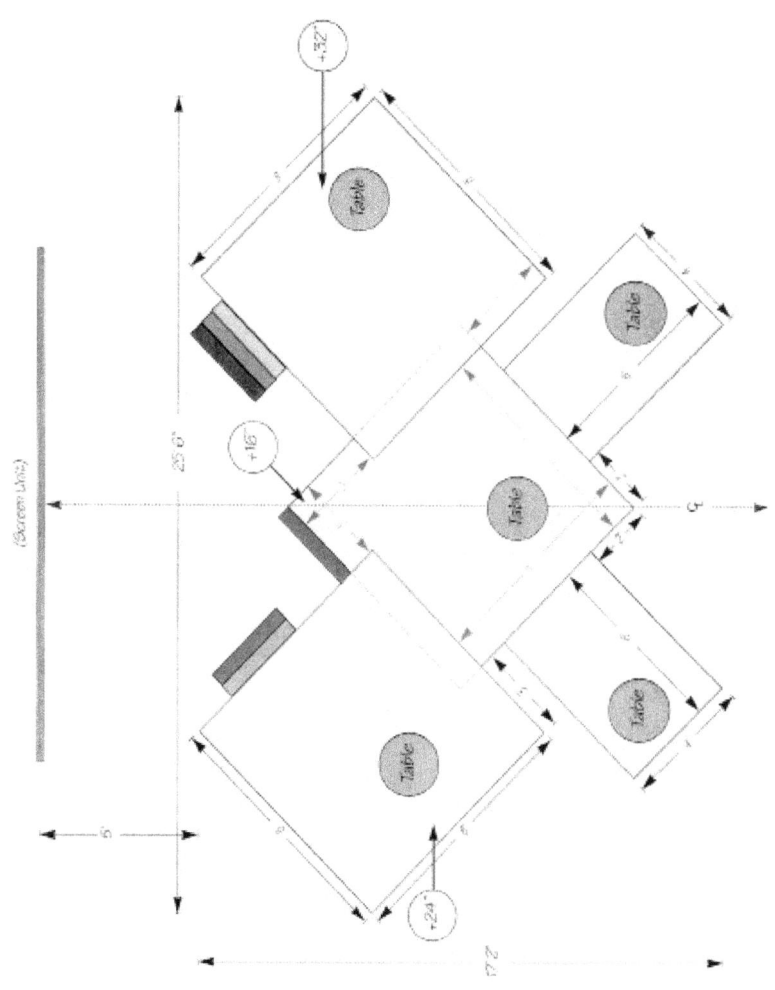

You've Got Hate Mail
Scale = 1/4"=1'

See what people are saying about
YOU'VE GOT HATE MAIL...

"The perfect bedroom farce!"
– *New York Post*

"It doesn't get better than this!"
– *Show Business*

"Outright guffaws!"
– Peter Filichia

"A FUNNY PLAY! The verbal zingers fly fast and furious!"
– *Asbury Park Press*

"LOL! The audience is guaranteed to do just that - LAUGH OUT LOUD!"
– *Star Ledger*

"HILARIOUS! RIOTOUS! I haven't enjoyed theater like this since the days of the late Charles Ludlum and his Ridiculous Theatrical Company! I CAN'T RECOMMEND THIS PLAY ENOUGH!"
– *CultureCatch.com*

Also by
Billy Van Zandt & Jane Milmore...

Bathroom Humor

Confessions of a Dirty Blonde

Do Not Disturb

Drop Dead!

Having a Wonderful Time, Wish You Were Her!

High School Reunion: the Musical

Infidelities!

Lie, Cheat, and Genuflect

A Little Quickie

Love, Sex, and the I.R.S.

A Night at The Nutcracker

Playing Doctor

The Senator Wore Pantyhose

Silent Laughter

Suitehearts

Till Death Do Us Part

What the Bellhop Saw

What the Rabbi Saw

Wrong Window!

Please visit our website **samuelfrench.com** for complete descriptions and licensing information.

OTHER TITLES AVAILABLE FROM SAMUEL FRENCH

WRONG WINDOW!

Billy Van Zandt & Jane Milmore

Comedy/Thriller / 5m, 3f / Interior

Van Zandt & Milmore pay tribute to Master of Horror Alfred Hitchcock, with this comedy whodunit. Off-and-on New York couple Marnie and Jeff enter an even more complicated phase of their relationship when they think they spy their cross-courtyard neighbor do away with his wife. After they draw their torn curtain, the lady vanishes, and suspicion places murder beyond a shadow of a doubt. The bumbling witnesses sneak into their neighbor's apartment - 39 steps away - and the fun begins. Among multiple door-slammings, body-snatchings, and a frantic flashlight chase scene, two questions remain: Who killed Lila Larswald? And… if she's not dead…then who is? The crazy farce plays out on a shadow-box set that allows the audience to be present in one apartment, while viewing the action in its mirror-image neighboring unit across the way. "Take the money and run to this window before it closes!" *Two River Times.*

"If you're a fan of *Rear Window* on screen, you'll award *Wrong Window* on stage a perfect 10. A barrage of gag-filled dialogue. Knee-slappingly funny from start to finish! Take the money and run to this window before it closes!"
– Philip Dorian, *Two River Times*

"Fever-pitched one liners, puns, slapstick, pratfalls…There are probably no people in America more adept at conveying these classic comic styles than Van Zandt & Milmore, with their wacky anything for a laugh adventuring and willingness to toss all actorly dignity out the window!"
– Tom Chesek, *Asbury Park Press*

SAMUELFRENCH.COM

OTHER TITLES AVAILABLE FROM SAMUEL FRENCH

LOVE, SEX, AND THE I.R.S.

Billy Van Zandt & Jane Milmore

5m, 3f / Int.

Here is a wild farce with twists of fate, sight gags, mistaken identities and hilarious comic lines. Jon Trachtman and Leslie Arthur are out of work musicians who room together in New York City. To save money, Jon has been filing tax returns listing the pair as a married. The day of reckoning comes when the Internal Revenue Service informs the "couple" they're going to be investigated by a Mr. Spinner. Leslie masquerades as a housewife, aided by Jon's fiancee, Kate. Complicating matters further Leslie and Kate are having an affair behind Jon's back, Jon's mother drops in unexpectedly to meet her son's fiancee, and Leslie's ex girlfriend shows up demanding to know why Leslie has changed and won't see her anymore. The premiere was at New Jersey's Dam Site Dinner Theatre.

"Enough comic lines to fill an encyclopedia of humor."
– *Red Bank Register*

The *Asbury Park Press* warned the diner to eat carefully before curtain time or "he might laugh enough to choke if he does not."

SAMUELFRENCH.COM

OTHER TITLES AVAILABLE FROM SAMUEL FRENCH

A NIGHT AT THE NUTCRACKER

Book and Lyrics by Billy Van Zandt & Jane Milmore
Music by Ed Alton

Selections from the Nutcracker Ballet
by Peter Tchaikovsky

7m, 5f (2 dancers) / Unit Set

Reminiscent of the screwball farces during the golden age of cinema, this romping musical teams Felix T. Filibuster, the greatest detective in the world, up with Pinchie the silent butler, and his Italian friend and coworker, Pepponi. The trio, along with a classic comedic cast, try to prove that Clyde Ratchette is trying to swindle the wealthy Mrs. Stuffington, who has just invested a bundle in the production of *The Nutcracker Suite*. The mishaps, jokes, musical numbers and mayhem lead to a farcical climax that incorporates elements of *The Nutcracker Suite* into its craziness. A guaranteed crowd pleaser.

OTHER TITLES AVAILABLE FROM SAMUEL FRENCH

THE PROPERTY KNOWN AS GARLAND

Billy Van Zandt

Comedy / 1m, 1f / Interior

Her talent is legendary. Her wit, sublime. Her true story more electrifying than you'd ever imagine. She is Judy Garland. Adrienne Barbeau starred in this fictional backstage account of Judy's final concert appearance. With her wicked wit, Judy dishes the dirt on her co-stars, ex-husbands, Mr. Mayer, and more- taking us down the rocky yellow brick road of her incredible life. An amazing tour-de-force.

"Thrilling!"
– *Variety*

"Remarkable!"
– *The New York Sun*

"More entertaining and insightful than most shows of its kind!"
– *The New York Blade*

"Garland fans wouldn't have it any other way!"
– *Associated Press*

SAMUELFRENCH.COM

www.ingramcontent.com/pod-product-compliance
Lightning Source LLC
Chambersburg PA
CBHW070650300426
44111CB00013B/2357